THE SIMPLE STRATEGY

A Powerful Day Trading Strategy
For Trading Futures, Stocks, ETFs and Forex

Markus Heitkoetter
Mark Hodge

The Simple Strategy

A Powerful Day Trading Strategy For Trading Futures, Stocks, ETFs and Forex. All Rights Reserved.

ISBN 10: 0692329242

ISBN 13: 9780692329245

PRINTED IN THE UNITED STATES OF AMERICA

Table of Contents

Chapter 1

How "The Simple Strategy" Can Help You in Your Trading

"The Simple Strategy" is a powerful trend-following strategy. It's very popular among traders because of the following benefits:

- **Clear Entry Rules**

  When trading **"The Simple Strategy"** there's no second-guessing. The entry rules are based on indicators - and these rules are black and white. MACD is above the zero line or it isn't. And either RSI is above 70 or it isn't. This makes entries easy to identify and execute. That's why this strategy is called **"The Simple Strategy."**

- **Clear Exit Rules**

  When trading **"The Simple Strategy"** you will know when to exit before you ever enter a trade. This means you will know exactly how much to risk on any given trade, which is essential for precise position sizing and money management. Plus, you can put the trade on auto-pilot once your entry order is filled, keeping trade management to a minimum. This is important because many traders fail by over-managing their trades. But with the exit rules of **"The Simple Strategy"** you won't have this problem. It's like the "Showtime Rotisserie" - You set it, and forget it :-)

- **Take advantage of small intraday trends**

  Low trading commissions and computerized trading have destroyed nice long intraday trends. The times when you

1

could enter the market in the morning and exit the market in the afternoon are over. These days trends are short-lived and the markets can turn on a dime. But with "**The Simple Strategy**" you can take advantage of the small intraday trends that we are seeing in today's markets. This is because we are only trying to capture 15% of the average daily range. More about this later.

- **You don't need sophisticated trading software**

    As you will see, you only need charting software that has "basic" charting capabilities. Your charting software needs to be able to plot RANGE BARS, BOLLINGER BANDS, MACD and RSI. More than 90% of the charting software packages that are available today have these options. So there's no need to buy any proprietary indicators or expensive charting software!

In short: **"The Simple Strategy"** will simplify your trading.

Using this strategy has helped ME tremendously in my own trading. Before I traded "**The Simple Strategy**," I was an indicator junkie. I plotted so many indicators on my chart that I could barely see price action any more. And all these indicators didn't help!

In fact, all of these indicators led to only ONE thing - Analysis Paralysis.

It's a common disease amongst traders - you analyze so many things and you become more confused. It happened to me! Looking at all the indicators on my screen, half of the indicators were indicating BUY and the other half were yelling SELL.

But then I discovered the powerful combination of just three indicators and **"The Simple Strategy"** was born.

No more ANALYSIS PARALYSIS. Clear entries and exits instead.

So let's get started...

Chapter 2

Can You Make Money If Half of Your Trades Are Losing Trades?

I have been using "**The Simple Strategy**" for many years now. It's one of my favorite trading strategies for a very simple reason: it is a trend following strategy.

As a trend-following strategy it has a positive risk-to-reward ratio. If you are trading "**The Simple Strategy**" according to its rules, you can expect to make $150 for every $100 that you risk.

In other words: You could have a winning percentage of only 50% and still make money with this strategy.

Let's look at an example:

Let's say you take 10 trades. Five of them are winning trades and five of them are losing trades. So you have a 50% winning percentage.

In this example you would make $750 on your five winning trades ($150 profit for each winning trade).

Winning Trades: $150 x 5 = $750

And you would lose $500 on your five losing trades ($100 loss on each losing trade).

Losing Trades: $100 x 5 = $500

So after 10 trades you're still making $250.

Total Profit $750 - $500 = $250

Even if you deduct $5 in commissions for each trade that you take ($5 x 10 trades = $50), you would still net $200. And that's with a measly 50% winning percentage!

In this book you will learn ways to identify the strongest trends and improve your winning percentage. And just for fun, let's look at what would happen if you managed a 60% winning percentage with this strategy.

In this case you would make 10 trades and have SIX winning trades and only FOUR losing trades.

You would make $900 on your six winning trades ($150 profit for each winning trade).

And you would lose $400 on your four losing trades ($100 loss for each losing trade).

Winning Trades: $150 x 6 = $900

Losing Trades: $100 x 4 = $400

Total Profit: $900 - $400 = $500

As a result, you would make $500 on 10 (hypothetical) trades. After estimated commissions, that's $450 in profits... not bad!

Chapter 3

What Makes "The Simple Strategy" So Powerful?

"The Simple Strategy" is so powerful because it's based on the reality of the markets. Using the strategy your job is to identify a trend and to ride the move for a short while. Then you need to get out before the trend runs out of steam.

You are NOT trying to pick bottoms and tops in the market because this simply doesn't work! At least not consistently.

When trading *"The Simple Strategy"* our goal is to ride a trend like a "hobo" would ride a train. We wait patiently until a train passes by. We then hop onto the train, ride it for a little while and then hop off.

We don't chase the train! We are not running behind the train trying to catch it after it left the station, and we're not on it for too long. We don't risk riding it into the next station and we don't wait for the train to stop. We only ride it for a short time while it's still moving. Then we get off the train before it comes to a halt.

All you need for *"The Simple Strategy"* is a short intraday trend. One you can jump on like a train for a quick ride before the market turns. You should get one at least once a day. And depending on the market, you might be able to get several trading opportunities a day.

Since *"The Simple Strategy"* is based on the reality of the markets, it works in ANY market: Stocks, ETFs, Futures or Forex.

That's why *"The Simple Strategy"* is so powerful.

Chapter 4

How To Set Up Your Charts For "The Simple Strategy"

Before we explain the exact rules of the strategy, let me show you how to set up your charts and indicators for trading "**The Simple Strategy**."

STEP 1: Select A Timeframe

"**The Simple Strategy**" is primarily used as a day trading strategy.

When displaying an intraday chart, you can select one of the following three options:

1) **Time-Based Charts**

   When choosing a time-based chart, you need to select a time interval like 1, 3, 5 or 15 minutes. You will then get a new bar or candle at the completion of your selected time interval. For example, a 5 minute bar completes and a new bar opens every 5 minutes. Time-based charts are common. But because they have many disadvantages, we prefer other methods for charting price action.

2) **Volume-Based Charts**

   When choosing a volume-based chart (a.k.a. tick chart) you need to select a volume threshold like 387 ticks. You will then get a new bar or candle every 387 trades. During active trading you will get more bars. And during times of low volume, like the overnight session, you'll get fewer bars.

7

This charting method is better than using time-based charts, but our preferred method is the THIRD option.

3) Volatility-Based Charts

When choosing a volatility-based chart (a.k.a. RANGE BAR) you need to select a volatility threshold or range, like 2 points. You will then get a new bar or candle when price moves MORE than the specified threshold. Using a 2 point range bar, you would get a new bar when price moves more than 2 points from the high OR the low of the bar. Although you can use "**The Simple Strategy**" on time-based or volume-based charts, we prefer to trade the strategy using RANGE BARS since this method has significant advantages over the other two types of charts.

IMPORTANT: We highly recommend using RANGE BARS when day trading "**The Simple Strategy**." If you need charting software that supports range bars, please check out our **Chapter 14: Resources** section of this book.

I personally like to trade "**The Simple Strategy**" on a variety of futures markets.

Here are the range bar settings for the markets I like to trade:

- *E-mini S&P (ES*) - 8 ticks or 2 points
- *E-mini Dow (YM)* - 18 ticks or 18 points
- *E-mini Russell (TF)* - 16 ticks or 1.6 points
- *EUR / USD (6E)* - 8 ticks or $0.0008
- *Gold (GC)* - 14 ticks or $1.40
- *Crude Oil (CL)* - 14 ticks or $0.14
- *30-year Bonds (ZB)* - 4 ticks or 4/32
- *10-year Notes (ZN)* - 2 ticks or 4/64

But as we said in the previous chapter: You can trade "**The Simple Strategy**" on ANY market. In **Chapter 6** we will explain how to determine range bar settings for other markets, e.g. stocks, ETFs and Forex.

STEP 2: Add Bollinger Bands - Indicator #1

Bollinger Bands are a great concept IF used correctly.

Bollinger Bands consist of a **Centerline** (which is a simple moving average), a standard deviation above the moving average (**Upper Bollinger Band**) and a standard deviation below the moving average (**Lower Bollinger Band**) – see picture 2.

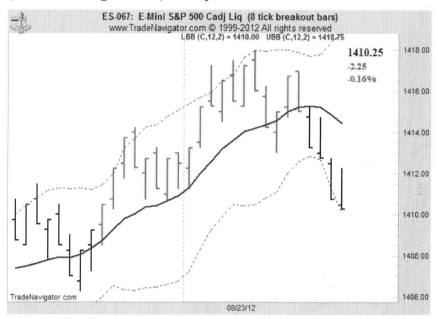

Picture 2: Bollinger Bands

When plotting the Bollinger Bands on your charting software, you need to specify the number of bars to use in the moving average and the standard deviation.

For "**The Simple Strategy**" we select **12 for the moving average and 2 for the standard deviation.**

Since we don't actually use the centerline for trading we remove it from our charts (see picture 3).

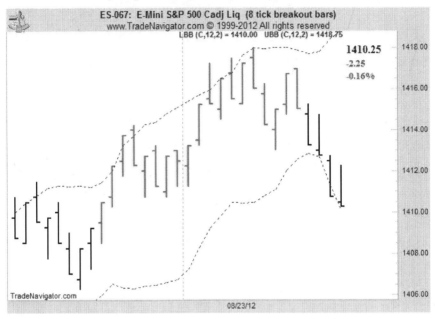

Picture 3: Bollinger Bands without Centerline

STEP 3: ADD Moving Average Convergence/Divergence (MACD) – Indicator #2

The second indicator that we use when trading "**The Simple Strategy**" is the Moving Average Conversion/Divergence (MACD).

The MACD consists of THREE components (see picture 4):

1) **The MACD itself**

The MACD is the difference between two exponential moving averages, a slow moving average and a fast moving average.

2) **The "Signal Line"**

The Signal Line is an exponential moving average of the MACD.

3) **The Histogram**

The histogram represents the difference between the MACD and the Signal Line. When the histogram is above the zero, then the MACD is above the Signal Line. And when the histogram is below the zero, then the MACD is below the Signal Line.

The histogram oscillates above and below a value of zero which is known as the "Zero Line".

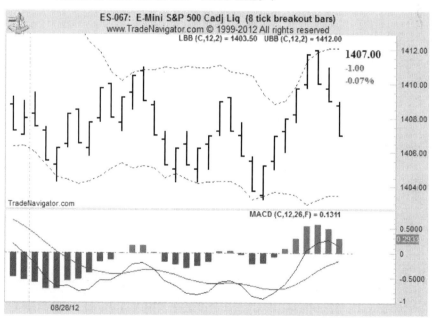

Picture 4: Moving Average Convergence Divergence (MACD)

For "**The Simple Strategy**" we select **26 for the slow moving average**, **12 for the fast moving average** and **9 for the signal line.**

When trading "**The Simple Strategy**" we like to color our charts based on the MACD:

- If the MACD is above the zero line AND above the signal line, we like to color our bars in **GREEN** - indicating BULLISH market conditions.

- If the MACD is below the zero line AND below the signal line, we like to color our bars in **RED** - indicating BEARISH market conditions.

Coloring the bars is optional, but it helps us quickly identify trading opportunities according to **"The Simple Strategy"** rules, making it easy to trade multiple markets (see picture 5).

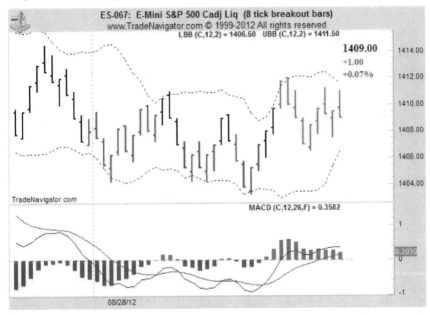

Picture 5: Coloring of bars based on MACD

The MACD alone does NOT give us an entry signal, but we start looking for BUYING opportunities (LONG trades) when the MACD is above the zero line and above the signal line, i.e. **GREEN** bars.

And we start looking for SELLING opportunities (SHORT trades) when the MACD is below the zero line and below the signal line, i.e. **RED** bars.

STEP 4: Add Relative Strength Index (RSI) – Indicator #3

The third indicator to plot when trading "**The Simple Strategy**" is the **Relative Strength Index (RSI)** developed by Welles Wilder (see picture 6). This indicator is optional as a strategy rule, but it can help traders identify stronger trends.

The RSI is an oscillator measuring the relative strength or weakness of a market. It oscillates between 0 and 100. The lower the RSI the weaker the market, and the higher the RSI, the stronger the market.

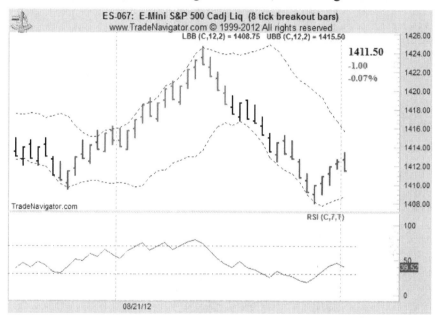

Picture 6: Relative Strength Index (RSI)

To calculate RSI you need ONE value – the number of previous bars it should use to identify the relative strength or weakness of a market.

For "**The Simple Strategy**" we use a **7 period setting for RSI.**

Just like we color the bars on the chart based on the MACD, we like to visually represent the value of the RSI using **Highlight Markers** on the chart (see picture 7)

- If the RSI is above 70, we like to place **GREEN TRIANGLES** below the bars.

- If the RSI is below 30, we like to place **RED TRIANGLES** above the bars.

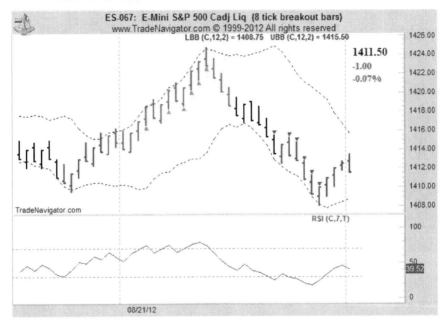

Picture 7: Highlight Markers based on RSI

Placing these highlight markers on the chart is OPTIONAL, but it helps us quickly determine the strength of a trend. "RSI Confirmation" can be used as a filter for identifying high-probability trade setups.

You shouldn't have any problems configuring your charts as outlines above. But if you need help, please contact us.

Chapter 5

The Rules of The Simple Strategy

Here are the exact rules of the strategy.

(1) Long Entry

1) **We must have Bullish Market Conditions based On MACD**:

   MACD must be ABOVE the signal line and ABOVE the zero line. If you are coloring your bars as suggested in **Chapter 4**, you want to see GREEN bars on the chart.

2) **AND Bollinger Bands must indicate an uptrend**:

   The Upper Bollinger Band needs to point up.

3) **RSI should be above 70 (OPTIONAL)***

   A 7 period RSI reading above 70 helps confirm the strength of the trend.

If these conditions are met, we **place a BUY STOP order** 1 tick above the high of the bar closing AT or NEAR the Upper Bollinger Band.

NOTE: RSI Confirmation & Filters

RSI can be used to help confirm the strength of a trend. We've found that when using a period of 7 for day trading, RSI readings above 70 are extremely bullish and RSI readings below 30 are extremely bearish. However, strong signals can occur before RSI actually gives a reading above 70 or below 30. For this reason we encourage traders to use RSI as a filter, and to decide based on experience and testing if it should be required as an entry rule.

Using RSI or any other indicators as a filter will limit the number of signals that can be traded. The goal of a filter is to improve the performance of the signal that is used to enter the market. However, there's no such thing as the perfect filter. Although a good filter will keep you out of losing trades, it will also keep you out of some winning trades as well.

Let's look at a BUY entry signal.

In this example we'll use my favorite market: **the e-mini S&P** (see screenshot below).

In later chapters we will show you some examples for trading stocks, ETFs and Forex with this strategy, but for now we'll stick to the e-mini S&P Futures.

As suggested in the previous chapter we are using 8 tick range bars.

Looking at the right-hand side of the chart you will notice that the green bar is preceded by 3 black bars. These bars are black because our rules are no longer valid for a downtrend, and only one of our conditions for an uptrend is present (MACD is greater than the Signal Line, but MACD is NOT yet greater than the Zero Line).

On the last bar the MACD pushed above the Zero Line and therefore both conditions for the MACD are met. According to our coloring the bar turns green (see picture 8).

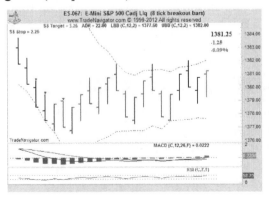

Picture 8: First Green Bar

The Upper Bollinger Band at this time is pointing up, but the current bar closes well below the Upper Bollinger Band. We are looking for a close AT or NEAR the Upper Bollinger Band.

The next bar closes even further away from the Upper Bollinger Band and the Upper Band is now pointing sideways (see picture 9). So we still don't have an entry signal.

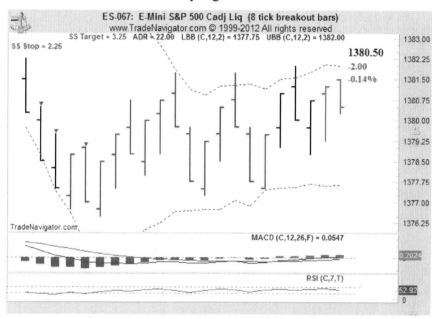

Picture 9: No Entry Signal Yet

One bar later the Upper Bollinger Band is pointing up again, but the bar does NOT close at or near the Upper Band (see picture 10). So, we have to wait for another bar.

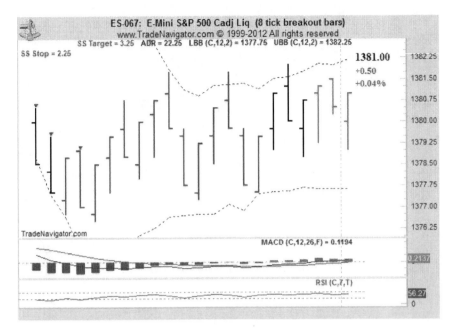

Picture 10: Waiting For A Close At The Upper Bollinger Band

Another bar finishes and closes at its low - far away from the Upper Bollinger Band (see picture 11). We need to be patient to get our entry signal.

Remember: We don't want to chase the market. The market has to do what WE want!

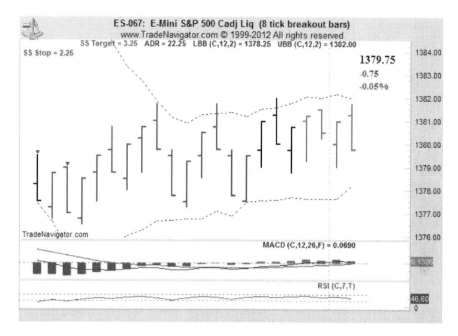

Picture 11: The Bar Closes At The Low

Another bar finishes and closes well below the Upper Bollinger Band. No entry... yet.

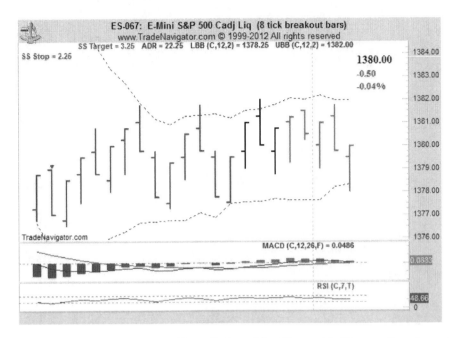

Picture 12: Another Close Below The Upper Bollinger Band

The next bar finally closes at the Upper Bollinger Band, and the band is pointing nicely up. The MACD has been above the zero line and above its Signal Line for the past 6 bars, all of them colored GREEN.

Therefore, our entry conditions are met and we place a BUY STOP order 1 tick above the high of the current bar. The high of the current bar is 1382.00; therefore we place our BUY STOP order at 1382.25 (see picture 13).

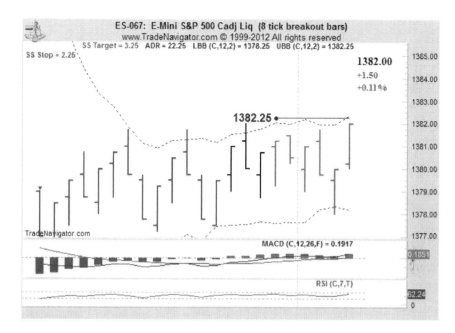

Picture 13: Entry with BUY STOP order at 1382.25

We are getting filled on the next bar (see picture 14). Now it's time to place the exit orders.

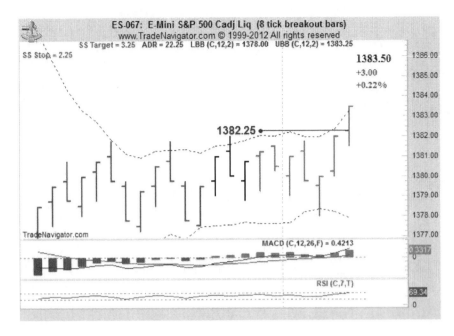

Picture 14: Filled at 1382.25

(2) Long Exit

THE AVERAGE DAILY RANGE

Our exits are based on the **Average Daily Range (ADR)**. The ADR measures how much a market is expected to move based on recent trading ranges.

To determine the ADR we begin with the daily range. The daily range is simply the high of the day minus the low of the day. To get the average of the range we take the daily range of the last seven trading days and divide by seven.

ADR = (Daily High – Daily Low)/7

The ADR lets us know what type of movement to expect based on recent market conditions. When there is less volatility and ranges are smaller, we will use a smaller profit target and stop loss to make sure that our exits are appropriate for current market conditions. When there is greater volatility and ranges are larger, we will use a larger profit target and stop loss.

NOTE: More and more traders are using the ADR, but it's not readily available in all charting packages. If your charting software doesn't offer the ADR you have 3 options:

1) Calculate the ADR by hand. Once you have the range of the last 7 trading days it's pretty easy to update the ADR each day and manually calculate the ADR.

2) If your software offers the ability to create a custom indicator you should be able to program the ADR using the calculation above. If you are interested in software that offers custom indicators and highlight features, please take a look at **Chapter 14: Resources**.

3) The Average True Range (ATR) indicator is not the same as the ADR, but it is similar in concept. If you have access to the ATR and don't want to program or manually calculate the ADR, the ATR can be used as a substitute

DETERMINING THE PROFIT TARGET AND STOP LOSS

We use the ADR to determine when to exit the market. We use 15% of the ADR as our Profit Target and 10% of the ADR as our stop loss.

In the previous Long Entry example the ADR is 22.25 points.

We place a **stop loss** at 10% of the ADR, rounded to the nearest tick:

$22.25 * 0.10 = 2.25$

Entry price $1382.25 - 2.25 = \mathbf{1380.00}$

So we place a **stop loss at 1380.00** (see picture 15)

Note: 1 point in the e-mini S&P is $50, so we are risking $112.50 per contract.

Next, we place an order to take profits if the trade moves in our favor.

Our profit target is 15% of the ADR, rounded to the nearest tick:

$22.25 * 0.15 = 3.25$

Entry price 1382.25 + 3.25 = **1385.50**

We place a **profit target at 1385.50** (see picture 15)

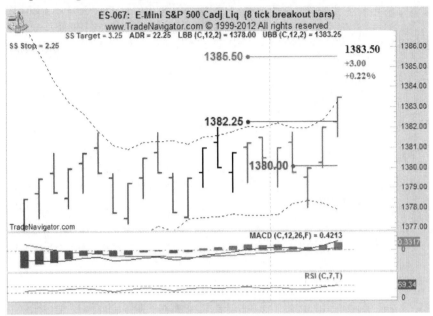

Picture 15: Exit Orders – Stop Loss And Profit Target

In this example we risk 2.25 points ($112.50 per contract) in an attempt to make 3.25 points ($162.50 per contract) if the trend continues.

The next bar closes higher at 1384.75 - just 3 ticks away from our profit target. We need another push higher to reach our target of a 3.25 points profit (see picture 16).

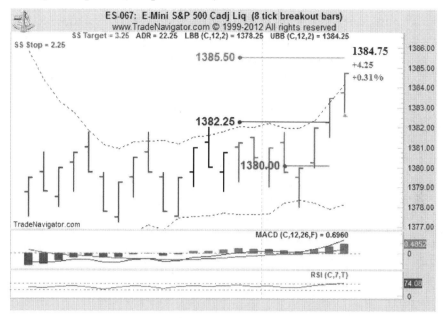

Picture 16: Profit Target In Sight

The next bar closes only one tick higher at 1385.00. We still need two more ticks until we arrive at our profit target (see picture 17).

Remember that we don't over-manage the trade! Our stop loss and profit target are in the market so we can patiently wait until either one gets filled.

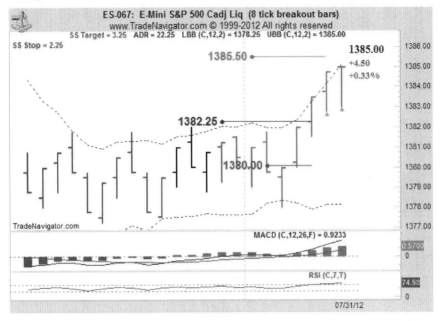

Picture 17: Only Two Ticks Away From Profit Target

On the next bar our profit target is filled and we make 3.25 points or $162.50 per contract traded (see picture 18).

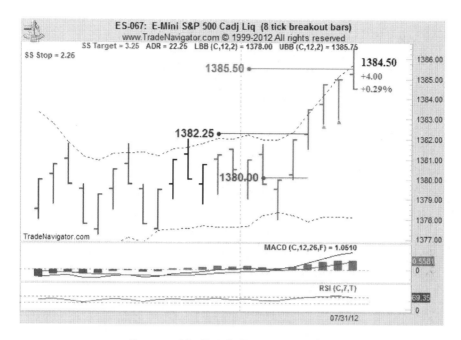

Picture 18: Profit Target Reached

Keep in mind that this trade could have been a losing trade. However, if it would have been a losing trade we would only lose $112.50 per contract since we limited our loss to 2.25 points.

As you can see in the chart below, prices moved a few ticks higher after our exit and then pulled back (see picture 19).

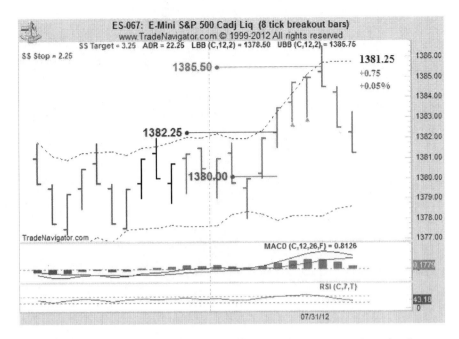

Picture 19: Prices Retrace After Profit Target Is Reached

In the end we left a few dollars on the table, but don't worry about it. You will NEVER catch the perfect exit. Whenever you exit a trade, it's either too early or too late.

That's why we like to work with profit targets. When using profit target we're not chasing the market. Instead we let the market come to us.

(3) Short Entry

1) Bearish Market Conditions Based On MACD:

MACD must be BELOW the signal line and BELOW the zero line. If you are coloring your bars as suggested in the previous chapter, you want to see RED bars on the chart.

2) Bollinger Bands need to indicate downtrend:

The Lower Bollinger Band needs to point down.

3) RSI less than 30 (OPTIONAL)

A 7 period RSI reading below 30 helps confirm the strength of trend.

If these conditions are met, then place a SELL STOP order 1 tick below the low of the bar closing AT or NEAR the Lower Bollinger Band.

Let's take a look at an example for a SHORT signal.

As you can see in the **e-mini S&P** chart below, the market has been moving sideways for a while. We had a few GREEN bars indicating bullish market conditions, but prices never closed at or near the Upper Bollinger Band, so there were no entries.

Now the MACD is below the zero line and below its Signal Line on the far right of the chart. We like to use this condition to color our bars RED, indicating BEARISH market conditions (see picture 20).

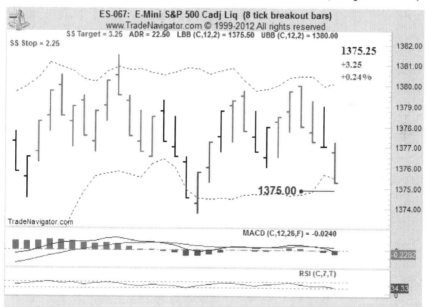

Picture 20: RED Bar Indicating Bearish Market Conditions

The current bar closes right at the Lower Bollinger Band. The close is at 1375.25 and we **place a SELL STOP order** to go short 1 tick below the low at 1375.00.

Note: If you want to wait another bar to confirm that the Lower Bollinger Band is really pointing down, you can do so. In this case you would go short at 1374.50 (see picture 21).

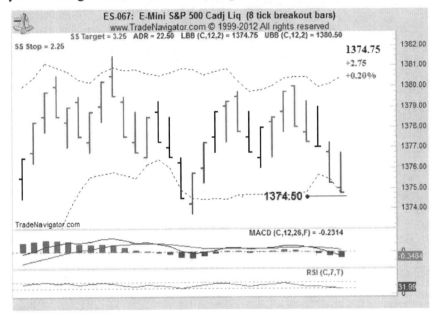

Picture 21: Short Entry After Waiting One More Bar

We get filled immediately at the open of the next bar and now we're short the e-mini S&P at 1374.50.

Now it's time to place our exit orders.

(4) Short Exit

When placing our short exit orders we use the same concept as previously described:

- Limit your loss to 10% of the Average Daily Range (ADR)
- Take profits at 15% of the Average Daily Range (ADR)

In this example the Average Daily Range of the e-mini S&P is 22.50.

We place a **stop loss** at 10% of the ADR, rounded to the nearest tick:

22.50 * 0.10 = 2.25

Entry price 1374.50 + 2.25 = **1376.75**

So we place a **stop loss at 1376.75** - 2.25 points above our entry price (see picture 22).

Note: 1 point in the e-mini S&P is $50, so we are risking $112.50 per contract.

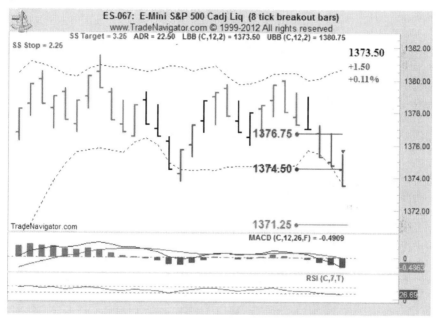

Picture 22: Placing Our Stop Loss

Next, we place an order to take profits if the trade moves in our favor.

Our profit target is 15% of the ADR, rounded to the nearest tick:

22.50 * 0.15 = 3.25

Entry price 1374.50 - 3.25 = **1371.25**

So we place a **profit target at 1371.25** (see picture 23).

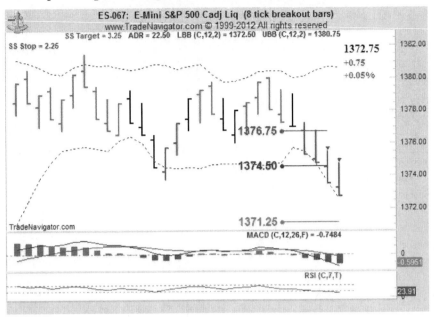

Picture 23: Prices Move Towards Our Profit Target

On the next bar prices move to our profit target which is 3.25 points or $162.50 per contract (see picture 24).

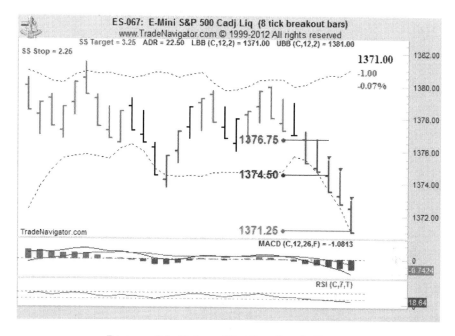

Picture 24: Prices Hit Our Profit Target

As you can see, the market continues to push a little bit lower before turning around. (see picture 25).

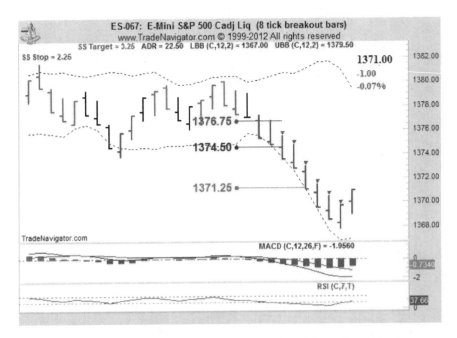

*Picture 25: The Market Moves A Few More Bars And
Then Turns Around*

We are leaving some money on the table, but that's fine. Remember: You will ALWAYS exit either too early or too late. You won't be able to catch the entire trend, and attempting to do so usually results in profits that are unnecessarily given back to the market. This is why it's easier to set your exits as soon as you enter the market and let the market do the rest!

We were able to extract some profits out of this short move and move on. The next trade is just around the corner.

Chapter 6

Determining Range Bar Setting For Other Markets

As we've shared, range bars offer a powerful way to view the markets. However, some testing and experience is necessary when determining the appropriate range bar size for markets that we don't trade regularly.

These are the steps we take when considering the appropriate range bar setting for new markets:

Step 1: Average the Average Daily Range (ADR) over the last 3-6 months

Market volatility and ranges can change. Although we find it unnecessary to adjust range bar settings every time there are small changes in volatility, it's good to know if the current range is "normal". Reviewing the ADR going back 30 days at a time will help to determine if the recent ADR is typical for the market being considered.

Example: Let's say that the E-mini Dow (YM) has the following ADR values:

> June 14th ADR = 252
> May 14th ADR = 138
> April 14th ADR = 157

With these values we can now determine an "average" ADR:

> $252 + 138 + 157 = 547/3 = 182.3$

Step 2: Start with 10% of the ADR

By definition, new range bars form whenever a specified range is exceeded. This means that large range bar settings will provide very few bars during the trading session, and small range bar settings will produce numerous bars. The problem with few bars is that you'll have limited trading opportunities, and signals might come late. A setting that generates too many bars can lead to false signals, and can also be extremely challenging to trade.

There is a "sweet spot" to look for when determining an appropriate range bar setting. In our testing and experience the best setting can vary from market to market, but is often found at around 10% of the Average Daily Range.

Example: *In Step 1 we calculated a simple average of the ADR over the last 3 months. 10% of this average is 18.2 (182.3 x .10 = 18.23). Rounding down, we can begin reviewing a range bar setting of 18 for this market.*

NOTE: Although we could skip step 1 and start with 10% of the current ADR to make things easy, we might be referencing an ADR that is much larger than normal. For example, if we started with 10% of the ADR on June 14th we would consider a range bar setting of 25 ticks (252 x .10 = 25.2). Although this range bar setting might be okay for current market conditions, there's a good chance that ranges will shift to a normal range, and another adjustment would be necessary in the future.

Step 3: Test Simple Strategy Signals

Regardless of how you go about determining the appropriate range bar setting for a market, the ultimate goal is to use a setting that keeps you out of sideways markets, and one that gives you signals to get into the market when trends are strong. The next steps are to review signals and to do some additional testing.

Remember that by using "**The Simple Strategy**" exit rules, you can be profitable with a 50% winning percentage! Since we know that it's unrealistic to have winning trades all of the time, we're really shooting for a setting that gets us into profitable trades 50-60% of the time. To make sure that signals are evaluated in different conditions, it's always good to test a minimum of 40 trades when experimenting with a new market. The more the better!

Chapter 7

Trading With Time Bars

It's important to make sure that you have the right tools to get the job done. If it's time to paint your house and all you have is a tiny paint brush, do you stick with what you have? You might be able to get by with a small paint brush, but you'll waste a lot of time and energy that could be saved with a little investment in the proper tools. The same can be said for charting software.

There is software that provides traders with the basics, and this is exactly what this software is intended to do. But you are trading against some of the fastest computers and smartest individuals in the world.

It's true that you don't need to be the smartest, or the most talented individual to make money in the markets. But you need to make sure that you can spot opportunities and execute your plan. Range bars offer a huge advantage over other types of charts when day trading, so make sure you have the right trading tools to trade your trading plan! The great thing is that range bars are now offered by most major charting packages.

Although range bars are our preference for day trading, the same type of signal can be considered when trading "**The Simple Strategy**" with time bars.

Strategy Considerations When Using Time Bars

A 5 minute chart is a great time period for day traders to start with when looking for Simple Strategy signals. However, markets tend to have their own personality and it never hurts to review signals on a 3 minute chart, and on a 10 or 15 minute chart as well. Do a little testing to make sure that the timeframe you are using gets you into the strongest trends, without too many false signals.

One big advantage with range bars with "**The Simple Strategy**" is that you are able to anticipate where the next bar will open. Since a bar completes and a new bar begins whenever a specified range is exceeded, you can place orders in the market and wait for the market to come to you. This isn't the case with time bars.

Using time bars, you are unable to anticipate where the next bar will open, or where the actual low or high of the bar will be while the bar is forming. For this reason it is important to wait for a time bar to complete in order to have a true signal. Once a bar has completed you can do one of two things:

(1) Place Entry Orders at the Bollinger Band

If a signal is valid but the close of the bar is inside of the Bollinger Bands, consider placing entry orders at the value of the Bollinger Band. For example, if there is a textbook Simple Strategy entry in an uptrend and the bar completes below the Upper Bollinger Band, place a Buy Stop order at the Upper Bollinger Band and wait for the order to be triggered. If the order is not filled and the bar completes, you have the option of adjusting the order if the signal is still valid. If market conditions have changed and the signal is no longer valid, you simply cancel the order and move on to new opportunities.

The same can be said for a downtrend. If there is a valid sell signal and the close of the bar is above the Lower Bollinger Band, place a Sell Stop order at the Lower Bollinger Band.

Let's look at an example of a Buy Signal...

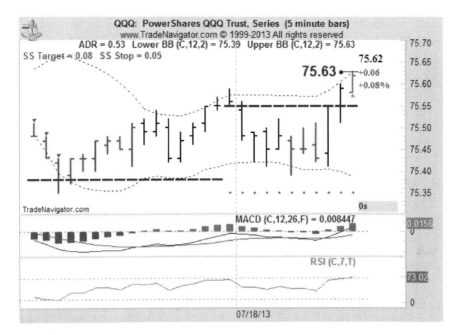

Picture 26: Buy Stop Order Placed At Upper Bollinger Band

In the chart above we have a 5 minute chart of QQQ. At the completion of the signal bar, the bar closes at 75.62 but the Upper Bollinger Band has a value of 75.63. Since the bar doesn't close at the Upper Bollinger Band you can use the Upper Bollinger Band as your entry point. This is done by placing a Buy Stop order at 75.63 to get into the trade.

With a move higher you would be filled around 75.63. Based on the Average Daily Range (ADR) of 53, your 10% ADR stop loss is 5 ticks at 75.58, and the 15% ADR target is 8 ticks at 75.71.

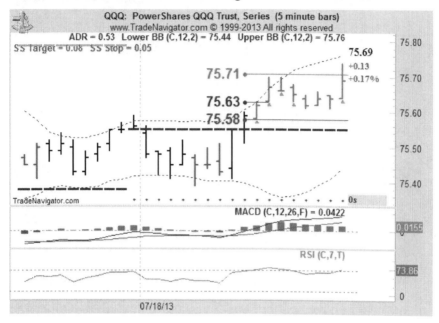

Picture 27: Our Profit Target At 75.71 Is Hit

(2) Use Market Orders to Enter

At times the bar will close at the Upper or Lower Bollinger Band, similar to a signal that would be considered when using range bars. In these cases you can simply enter a trade using a Market Order.

Let's look at some examples...

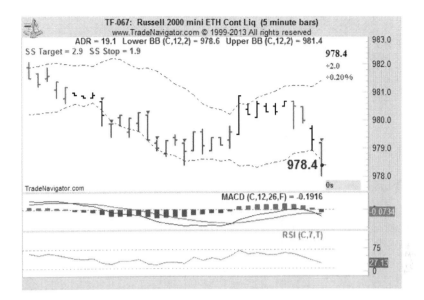

Picture 28: Sell Signal With Market Order Entry

In the chart above the bar closes below the Lower Bollinger Band (the Lower Band has a value of 978.6, and the actual close of the bar is 978.4). If the bar closed above the Lower Bollinger Band you could place a Sell Stop order at the Lower Bollinger Band. However, since the completion of the bar is two ticks below the Lower Bollinger Band, a SELL Market order is used to immediately enter the trade.

NOTE: Whenever there is a valid signal that closes at the Bollinger Band, or outside of the Bollinger Bands, the easiest way to enter the market is with a market order when using time bars.

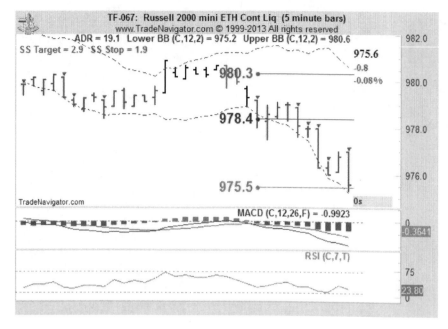

*Picture 29: Profit Target & Stop Loss Based
On Market Order Entry*

The same type of entry can be considered in uptrends...

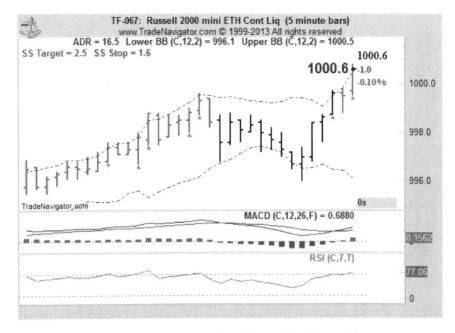

Picture 30: Buy Signal With Market Order Entry

In the chart above we see that a valid buy signal occurs when price clearly tags the Upper Bollinger Band. With an Upper Bollinger Band value of 1000.5 and the bar closing at 1000.6 we can submit a BUY Market order to get into the trade.

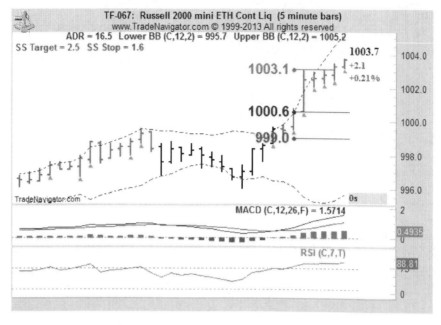

Picture 31: Profit Target & Stop Loss Based On 1000.6 Entry

NOTE: Slippage (the difference between your expected entry and actual fill) can occur when using market orders to enter the market. If we experience a fill that is worse than expected, our stop loss and profit target should always be based on the actual fill price, not the entry price we had hoped for.

Chapter 8

How to Trade Forex with "The Simple Strategy"

The same rules discussed in Chapter 5 apply when trading "**The Simple Strategy**" with Forex.

1. Determine the underlying direction of the market using MACD.

2. Look for buy & sell signals when price is tagging the Upper & Lower Bollinger Bands, using the Bollinger Band as an entry signal.

3. Determine the Average Daily Range and place your stop loss at 10% of the ADR and profit target at 15% of the ADR

Fortunately more and more Forex charting platforms are now giving traders the ability to plot range bars. If your charting software doesn't offer range bars consider upgrading to software that does, or use time bars as an alternative.

Let's look at an example of a long entry in the **$EUR-USD** using a 5 minute chart.

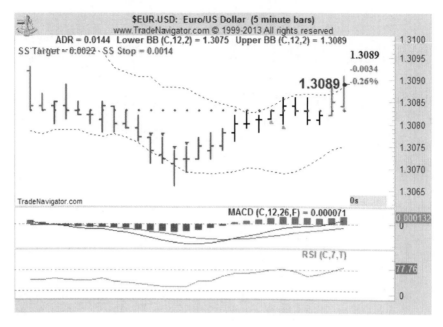

Picture 32: Entry At Upper Bollinger Band With Buy Market Order

Here we have a 5 minute chart of the $EUR-USD. In this example the 5 minute bar closes right at the Upper Bollinger Band. In this case we'll use a BUY Market Order to enter the market. Assuming that are entry was exactly at 1.3089 we'll now enter our profit target and stop loss based on the average daily range.

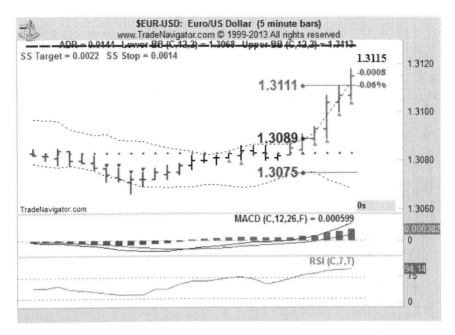

Picture 33: Buy Market Triggered With Move Higher

On this trading day the Average Daily Range (ADR) is 144 pips. Our stop is placed 14 ticks below our entry (based on 10% of the ADR). Our profit target is placed 22 ticks above our entry (based on 15% of the ADR).

Keep in mind that if our entry is higher than 1.3089 based on the bid/ask spread quoted by your broker, the stop loss and profit target should be adjusted and should always be based on the actual fill.

Let's look at an example in the **$JPY-USD...**

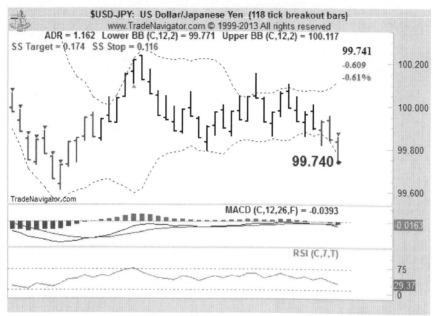

Picture 34: Simple Strategy Entry Order in $USD-JPY

Using 10% of the Average Daily Range as our range bar size (**see Chapter 6: Determining Range Bar Settings For Other Markets**), we plot the $USD-JPY chart using a 118 range bar setting. With a valid Simple Strategy sell signal we place a Sell Stop order at 99.741, 1 tick below the low of the bar.

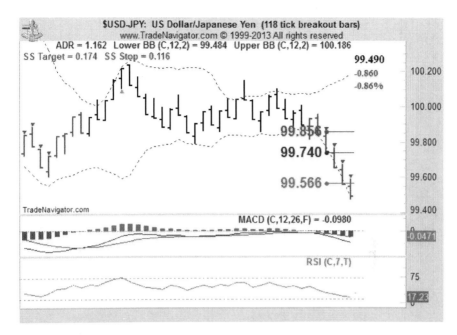

Picture 35: Simple Strategy Exits in $USD-JPY

After getting filled we are short $USD-JPY. Based on the current ADR of 1.162, our stop loss is .116 (10% of the ADR), and our target is .174 (15% of the ADR). As the market continues to move lower our profit target is met.

Chapter 9

How to Trade Stocks and ETFs with The Simple Strategy

We personally prefer to trade "**The Simple Strategy**" in leveraged markets. This is because we're able to control relatively large positions with as little as $500. When trades are successful, leverage magnifies returns and makes small intraday moves very attractive. Of course leverage is a double-edged sword, which means the greater the potential reward due to leverage, the greater the risk.

If you prefer stocks & ETFs over leveraged markets, you can trade "**The Simple Strategy**" with the following considerations:

(1) CONSIDER GAPS

A gap is the difference between the previous day's close, and the current trading session's open. Gaps occur because of market moves that happen in overnight trading. If you are using a 24 hour chart you will see what happened overnight, and more importantly, the indicators you use will include the most recent market moves in their calculations.

If you are trading a chart that only shows trades during the U.S session (typical for stock charts), your indicators at the open of the session are going to be calculated using the previous day's trading data. Since signals after a gap are based on data from the previous trading session, and not overnight moves, strategy entry signals after a gap can be somewhat misleading.

To further complicate things, many traders place trades with the expectation that a gap is likely to fill. This activity results in greater indecision and uncertainty at the open of the trading session.

For these reasons, the following filters and rules should be considered when trading stocks & ETFs:

- **Skip trades when a gap is GREATER than your stop loss.**

  If the gap is greater than your stop loss, consider waiting for a black bar before entering a trade. A black bar represents indecision or a possible change of direction. If a black bar occurs after a gap, the next signal is usually a stronger entry and a sign that a trend is likely to continue.

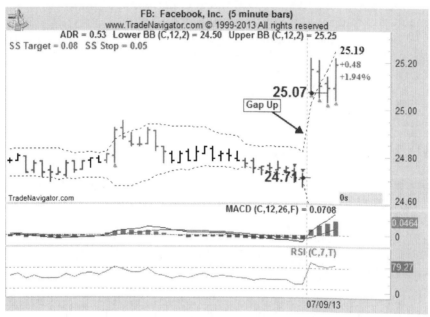

Picture 36: Facebook Gaps Higher At The Open

In the chart above **Facebook (FB)** has gapped up 36 cents. Based on the current ADR the stop loss is calculated at 5 cents. In a situation like this, a small attempt by the market to fill the gap will easily stop you out. Instead of entering on the first buy signal, wait for a black bar and look for another trend.

- **Consider trades after a gap has filled.**

  If the gap is smaller than your stop loss, or the gap is filled during the trading session, consider your standard Simple Strategy signals. In these situations a trend has a better chance of taking off since there is less pressure from traders to try and fill a gap.

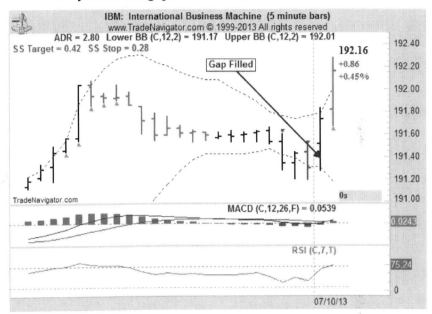

Picture 37: Gap Is Filled On The First Bar Of the Session

  In the chart above you'll notice that the very first bar of the session (the black bar 2nd from the right) fills the gap when the low of the bar is equal to or less than the previous session's close. After a gap fill the next entry signal can be considered.

- **Disregard gaps when the first bar of the session is a reversal bar (aggressive).**

  A reversal bar occurs when a market gaps higher, and then closes below the open of the first bar of the session. This is the opposite when a market gaps lower (close is higher than the open on the first bar of the session). In these scenarios you'll often find pressure for the market to fill the gap, which eliminates the possibility of a Simple Strategy signal. If the market has enough strength to reverse course and push right back through session highs or lows after a reversal bar, this is a pretty good sign of a trend. Although this setup is more aggressive than waiting for a black bar or for the gap to fill, there are some nice entries to consider when a valid Simple Strategy signal occurs following a reversal bar.

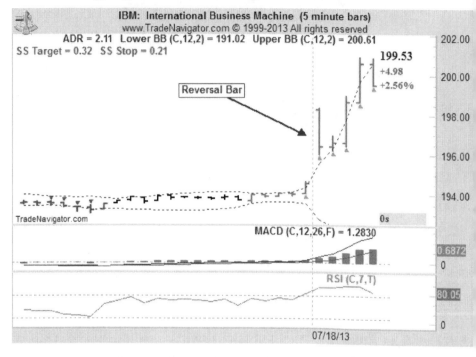

Picture 38: Market Gaps Higher Then Closes Lower on First Bar (Reversal Bar)

In the chart above you'll notice that IBM gaps up at the beginning of the trading session. Since the first bar of the session completes with a close below the open, we have a reversal bar. Aggressive traders can consider the next valid Simple Strategy entry signal.

(2) MODIFIED ENTRY RULE FOR STOCKS

When trading stocks with range bars, the standard entry rules apply (see chapter 5). However, if you are using time bars you won't be able to "anticipate" where the bar will close. In Chapter 7 (Trading With Time Bars) we discussed ways to enter Simple Strategy trades using time bars and the actual Bollinger Band as an entry point. These same considerations can be used when trading stocks, but some traders prefer the breakout method discussed below.

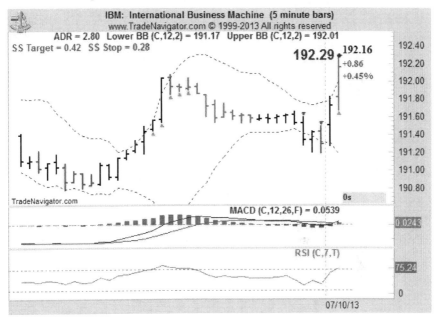

Picture 39: Buy Stop Placed 1 Cent Above High Of Bar

In the example above the first 5 minute bar of the session closes at 129.28. Instead of simply entering with a Market Order (as discussed in Chapter 7), A BUY STOP order is placed at 192.29, one cent above the high of the bar. If the market moves through our order we will enter the trade. If the market moves lower and the entry is no longer valid, we will cancel our order.

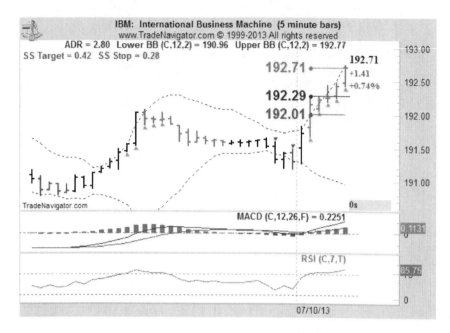

Picture 40: Buy Stop Ordered Triggered

In the chart above you will see that the market moves higher and our Buy Stop order is triggered. Let's assume that we have a fill at 192.29. Based on the ADR our profit target is .42 and our stop is .28. Using these values we place our target at 192.71 and our stop at 192.01

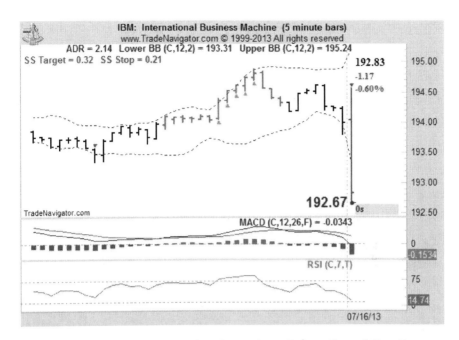

Picture 41: Sell Stop Order Once Cent Below Signal Bar Low

In a downtrend the same rules apply. Instead we will place a Sell Stop order 1 tick below the low of the bar. In this example the bar closes at 192.83 and the low of the bar is 192.68. Based on the breakout entry we place our Sell Stop order 1 tick below the low of the bar at 192.67.

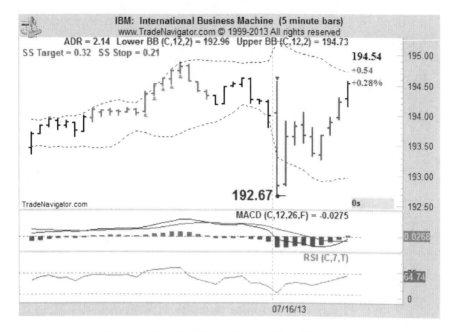

Picture 42: Sell Stop Order Not Triggered

You'll see the advantage of the breakout entry in the chart above. Unlike the previous example where our order is filled on the breakout, in this example our 192.67 SELL STOP order is never triggered as the market moves higher. The breakout entry will keep you out of trades when the market turns, but you'll sacrifice a better entry price at times.

Chapter 10

Simple Strategy Swing Trading

If you know me by now, you probably know that I LOVE range bars, and prefer to day trade the futures markets using "**the Simple Strategy**". However, I'm constantly being asked if this strategy works on daily charts and I want to share some ideas and tips that I've learned from other traders that have used this method to swing trade the markets.

Tip #1 – Cleanup Your Charts

If you've setup your charts and added daily support & resistance levels, you can clean your charts up by removing these levels. Instead focus more on MACD & Bollinger Bands. Switching to daily charts you'll probably find that it's best to keep things simple, using MACD to determine the direction of the market, and using Bollinger Bands to determine the best entries.

Tip #2 – Trade Stocks That Move, But Aren't "Gappy"

If you're scanning for stocks daily, you probably know exactly what I mean. There are some stocks that simply don't trend much, and instead spend time oscillating in ranges. We'll save how to trade this type of stock for another time, but for now...avoid rangebound stocks!

If you're a big fan of ETFs and small cap stocks, be careful of ETFs & stocks that have low volume and have big price gaps from one trading session to the next. These big gaps make it very difficult to swing trade.

Tip #3 – Focus On Signals When Price Tags The Bollinger Band

We discussed the importance of the slope of the Bollinger Band and the price bar closing at or near the band for an entry signal. When trading stocks be PICKY! Look for signals where the daily price bar actually tags the Upper or Lower Bollinger Band. You can then place a buy stop order 1 tick above the high of the signal bar in an uptrend, or 1 tick below the low of the signal bar in a downtrend. If the market gaps in the opposite direction you won't be filled and can cancel your order.

Tip #4 – Consider Adjusting Your Exit Rules

Although 10% of the ADR for a stop loss and 15% of the ADR for a profit target is great for day trading, swing traders need to allow more room to move. I've been told that the full ADR can be used as a decent stop loss. Instead of the 1:1.5 risk/reward ratio that we use for day trading, shoot for 1:2.

As an example, the current ADR for SPY is $2.40, if there is an entry signal consider a $2.40 stop loss and a $4.80 profit target.

Also watch MACD crossovers when you are in a trade! Remember that according to "**The Simple Strategy**," an uptrend or downtrend based on our MACD rules must be met. When day trading you'll rarely encounter times when a crossover in the opposite direction occurs before a profit target or stop loss is hit (a crossover occurs if MACD moves below the Signal Line in an uptrend, or MACD moves above the Signal Line in a downtrend, a condition represented by black bars on our charts). But crossovers are more likely to happen when using daily charts. I would consider a crossover a possible change of direction, and would treat this as an exit rule.

Tip #5 – Consider Inverse ETFs Or Puts For Short Signals

One of the best things about trading futures is that it is EASY to go short the market and profit form a move to the downside. This isn't always the case with stocks since shares need to be borrowed to short. It can be very frustrating when a great trade is missed because of a rejected order!

To combat this issue, consider trading inverse ETFs. If you're new to this concept, these are ETFs that move opposite the benchmark index. So you can actually buy an inverse ETF and be in a profitable trade if the benchmark index is going down!

As an example, if there is a short signal in the QQQ (NASDAQ 100), pull up the inverse ETF which is QID and look for a buy signal. If there is a short signal in the S&P 500, pull up the inverse ETF which is SH to look for a buy signal. This way you can enter a long position and benefit from the benchmark index moving lower, without missing out because of short restrictions or fill issues. Better yet, if you're familiar with options, consider buying a put and take advantage of the leverage!

Chapter 11

What To Expect When Trading The Simple Strategy

"**The Simple Strategy**" is a trend-following strategy with a risk-reward ratio of 1:1.5.

As we discussed earlier, a winning percentage of 50% is enough to make money with this strategy. And that's your initial goal: Strive for a 50% winning percentage.

With a little bit of practice and skill, you might be able to push this winning percentage even higher - maybe towards 60%. Don't expect miracles. Instead, aim for consistency. Once you are CONSISTENTLY profitable, you can use Money Management to increase your contract size and turbo-charge your account.

On average you can expect ONE signal according to "**The Simple Strategy**" per day per market. Keep in mind that we need a TREND in order to trade this strategy.

Many traders say that markets are only trending 20% of the time. I don't know if THAT is the exact number, but based on my experience markets are moving sideways most of the time. So, you have to be patient and wait for the right opportunity.

Chapter 12

Pitfalls and How to Avoid Them

As stated in the previous chapter, you need to be patient. Don't force a trade. Wait until everything lines up perfectly.

I highly recommend that you practice the strategy as follows:

1. Setup Your Charting Software

Configure your charting software as outlined in **Chapter 5**. If you don't have charting software yet, you should check out Genesis Trade Navigator. We are using this charting software package in our own trading. It's very powerful, yet inexpensive. You can download a 30 day free trial here: http://www.tradenavigator.com/rockwell. exe (**PC Only**) And let me know if you need help configuring your charting software. We have experience with several charting software packages including:

- TradeNavigator
- TradeStation
- ThinkOrSwim
- NinjaTrader
- AT Charts
- SierraCharts
- eSignal
- MultiCharts and others.

2. Identify Signals On Your Charts

After configuring the charts, try to identify signals according to "**The Simple Strategy**". If needed, print out the charts and mark the entry and exit signals on the printout. With a little practice you'll be able to spot that "perfect" signal with ease.

3. Backtest the Strategy

Once you get familiar with "**The Simple Strategy**" rules, it's time to back-test it. Start 30 days in the past and walk through the charts bar by bar. Identify entry signals and mark the exit signals. **Keep a trading log** of your back-tested trades so that you get your own performance statistics including important key metrics like **gross profit, profit per trade, winning percentage, profit factor, maximum drawdown, etc.**

4. Trade The Strategy On A Simulator (FORWARD TESTING)

After you have back-tested the "**The Simple Strategy**" on at least 40 trades, it's time to start the **Forward Testing**. You should now watch the markets LIVE and try to identify trading opportunities in real-time market conditions. Get familiar with entering orders on your trading simulator. You should practice entering both ENTRY orders and EXIT orders. Get familiar with the features of your trading platform before you start trading with real money. If you need a realistic simulator, check out the following simulator:

http://www.infinityfutures.com/practiceaccount.aspx?ref=rock.

This simulator is very realistic. And the best thing is… it's free!

And here are a few more tips when trading "**The Simple Strategy**":

- **Don't Trade Around Major Economic News Releases**

    Often the markets are bouncing erratically up and down after a major news release. We recommend that you don't trade 5 minutes before and after a major release. If you are in a position, you should consider exiting a position before the release. You can always re-enter if the trend continues. You can find a schedule for all major news releases here: www. ForexFactory.com

- **Don't Trade Into Major Support And Resistance**

  Don't enter a long position into major resistance and don't go short right into support. Often prices bounce off support and resistance levels therefore; you might get stopped out before the trend continues. Make sure that there are no support or resistance levels in the way between your entry and your profit target. We consider the following price points important support and resistance zones:

  o Pivot Points incl. S1, S2, R1 and R2,

  o The high of the previous day and

  o The low of the previous day

"**The Simple Strategy**" is a very mechanical strategy. It requires very little discretion. With a little bit of practice you will be able to easily spot trading opportunities on your chart.

The mechanical approach of this strategy is very helpful for traders who suffer from "analysis paralysis." When trading "**The Simple Strategy**", there's no second-guessing. Either the MACD is above the zero line and it's Signal Line, or it isn't. And either the Upper Bollinger Band is pointing up or it isn't. It's very black and white.

Many traders who use "**The Simple Strategy**" have said that they are more relaxed with their trading now. Especially since they can be wrong every other time and still make money. If you follow the rules of the strategy, you should make more money on your winning trades than you lose on your losing trades. So you don't need a ridiculously high winning percentage! A winning percentage of only 50% is a VERY achievable goal for most traders.

Another major advantage of "**The Simple Strategy**" is that the strategy is SELF ADJUSTING. By using exits based on the Average Daily Range you will have larger profit targets and stop losses when markets are more volatile. During quiet times you will have smaller profit targets and stop losses.

Since the profit targets and stop losses are not fixed, you can apply this strategy to any market.

"**The Simple Strategy**" is not curve-fitted to any market. It's based on the "universal laws" of the markets. You are not trying to pick bottoms and tops. You simply wait until the market starts trending, and then you ride the trend and get out before the trend ends.

Keep in mind that markets move sideways most of the time. Therefore you have to be patient and wait for the RIGHT opportunity. Be picky! Only enter trades when everything lines up perfectly.

Follow the mantra **"When in doubt, stay out!"**

If a bar closes too far away from the Bollinger Band, wait for another bar. If the Upper Band is not yet pointing up when you consider a long trade, wait another bar.

You should expect 1-2 trading signals according to this strategy per day. However, there will be days when you don't see any trading signals. That's fine. Don't force a trade.

If you are looking for more trading action, add another trading strategy to your trading plan. I'm usually using 3-4 different trading strategies: Two trend-following strategies for trending markets and one scalping strategy that I like to use in sideways markets. I like trading action; therefore I trade multiple strategies on multiple time frames.

Chapter 13

The Next Step

The next step is easy, yet the most difficult one for most people:

TAKE ACTION!

Don't let this book become another dusty book on your bookshelf. Take the steps outlined in **Chapter 12: Pitfalls and How To Avoid Them** and start using this strategy.

It's my sincere wish for you to achieve your trading goals and become the trader you want to be.

I hope this strategy helps you in your trading.

Chapter 14

Resources

(1) FREE DVD "The Simple Strategy"

The perfect addition for this eBook: Get a free DVD with more examples, tips and tricks for "The Simple Strategy: http://www. rockwelltrading.com/free-dvd-simple-strategy/

(2) FREE eBook "The Complete Guide to Day Trading"

If you are rather new to trading and would like to know more about the fascinating world of day trading, then you should get this book. It's 296 pages and you can download it for free from our website: http://www.rockwelltrading.com/ebook

(3) FREE Infinity AT Charts and Trade Simulator

If you would like to practice this strategy live and in real-time, you should download the Infinity AT Simulator and Charts. They're free for 30 days and one of the most realistic simulators that I know of:

http://www.infinityfutures.com/practiceaccount.aspx?ref=rock

(4) Rockwell Trading Indicators

After reading this eBook you should know how to set up your charting software for trading **"The Simple Strategy**." However, if you don't want to mess around with your software and would prefer to simply load our indicators with all of the strategy settings, you can go here: http://www.rockwelltrading.com/rockwell-indicators/

The indicators are available for the following charting software packages:

- AT Charts
- Genesis Trade Navigator
- TradeStation
- ThinkOrSwim
- NinjaTrader
- SierraCharts
- eSignal

Chapter 15

About The Author

Hi, I'm Markus Heitkoetter, and I have fulfilled my dream: I am living the lifestyle I want to live, can afford to buy the things I want and have more time for the things that are really important to me.

But it hasn't always been like this. Here's how it all started:

I was always fascinated by trading. In fact, I did my first trade when I was still in High School. I invested all the "risk capital" I had and **bought one share of Volkswagen (VW)**, a German car manufacturer. I think it cost me 50 Deutschmark, which is approximately $50. There I was: Proud owner of my first stock.

This was back in 1989, and I didn't have a cell phone. I don't know if cell phones even existed! And I didn't have a computer with real time data. At that time, my computer was a Commodore 64, with NO charting capabilities. So I called my broker at least twice a day and asked, "how much money did I make?"

On the third day my broker asked: "Markus, how much money do you want to make on this trade?" - I thought for a few seconds, and said "I would like to make $10, because that would mean I made 20% on my initial investment." - He said "Done! Come to my office tomorrow and I'll give you $10, but STOP CALLING ME."

So that was my first trade and it was a profitable one!

But I realized that I didn't have enough capital to really make a living day trading, so I went to college, got a Bachelor's Degree in Business

75

and Computer Science, and started a career. I climbed the corporate ladder very quickly, and at the age of 33, I was about to become the youngest Vice President of IBM in Germany. Life was good: I was responsible for IBM Global Services in Europe, Middle East and Africa (EMEA), I traveled across Europe and the Middle East, flew business class, rented luxury cars, became a Platinum Member for major airlines, car rentals and hotels, and was enjoying life in the fast lane.

In 2001, Everything Changed

But the corporate life was taking a toll on me: I was working 6 days a week and only at home for just hours on the weekend. Often I came home on a Saturday and left on Sunday. I had no time for friends, family, or the things that are really important in life. I realized I was stuck in the corporate rat race.

And in April 2000, the Internet Bubble burst. Working for IBM Global Services became more and more challenging, and in July 2002, IBM announced the purchase of Price Waterhouse Coopers Consulting (PWC) and the merger between IBM Global Services and PWC. And we all know what "merging" means!

The Decision

I decided it was time to get out of the corporate rate race and pursue my true passion: Trading!

While working for IBM, I was able to save some money and should be able to survive for a year without any income.

But the changes would be radical:

I needed to change my lifestyle: I would have to move into an apartment, sell my nice German car, and buy a used and cheaper one, eat in instead of dining in fancy restaurants, no more traveling ... even clipping coupons! But I was determined: I wanted to get out of the corporate rat race and become a trader.

In September 2002, I left IBM, sold a lot of my stuff, packed a few boxes, a bed, a table, four chairs and moved from Germany to the USA.

The Search

While working for IBM and living in hotel suites, I had been reading many books on day trading. I bought expensive software and since I had a degree in Computer Science, I even started developing my own day trading systems. Now I needed to make trading my profession, my source of income, and so I bought more day trading courses, books, systems, ... and spent most of my day in front of my computer.

It was grueling. Most things didn't work! I kept trying and trying, but my results were not matching my efforts!

I'm Ready to Give Up!

I was ready to give up!

I already spent a fortune on courses, seminars and books. I have been working hard and put many hours into my trading adventure. I'm not lazy, and I don't think I'm stupid. But at that point I just didn't know what to do or what to believe any more.

My trading account was not going anywhere: I made some money and I would lose some more. The account was dwindling down, and I'm bleeding to death. And my wife has news for me: She is pregnant.

In April 2003, my son Julius was born six weeks early and in his first days and weeks on earth he's battling all sorts of problems, and our medical bills were piling up. I was running out of funds quickly!

The three of us lived in an apartment that is barely furnished. What a difference! A year ago I was living the life in the fast lane, and now my decision to become a full time trader is severely impacting my family's life. But not as I thought it would: I COULDN'T afford to buy the things I wanted - heck, I could barely buy the things we needed. I spent most of my time in front of my computer, trying to make it work!

But I had to face reality: My day trading was not producing any income.

It seemed as though my career as a trader was done. I would probably have to go back and work for IBM again, in a different position and with a much smaller salary, since IBM had started laying off employees because of the merger with PWC.

The Breakthrough

With my back against the wall, I began to realize that I had to think differently.

Instead of trying to make $10,000 per month, I needed to focus on the next trade. Make $100. Then another $100. I started to focus on consistency instead of windfall profits. I realized that once I become consistent, I could increase the number of contracts I was trading, and instead of making $100 on a trade, I would make $200, then $300, ... $500... $1,000. I needed to start small, and then use Money Management to grow big.

My Epiphany

I realized that there is no Holy Grail, no day trading system or day trading robot that you can buy for $97 that will make you rich.

And I learned that as a trader, you need three essential skills:

1. **Determine the direction of the market.**
   Go with the flow! If the market is going up, buy. If the market is going down, sell. And if the market is going sideways, stay on the sidelines to avoid getting chopped into pieces. Being able to identify the direction was crucial to my trading!

2. **Know when to exit a position.**
   Use a stop loss, and use profit targets! Often I was in a winning trade, but I didn't take profits off the table while they were there. And so I let a winning trade turn into a

loser. Then I started using profit targets, and it made a huge difference in my trading. My profit targets were larger than my stop losses, and therefore the average winning trade was bigger than the average losing trade. That meant that I would be profitable if I "only" had a winning percentage of 50%. THIS epiphany took a lot of pressure off me.

3. **Use Money Management to grow your account.**
   Use proper risk, trade and money management! It has been proven again and again that poor money management will wipe out your trading account EVEN IF you have a profitable trading strategy! I realized that I had no idea about money management and that THIS ignorance cost me a lot of money. I analyzed my past trades and discovered that I could have done MUCH if I had used proper money management!

I finally got it!

I found an easy way to determine whether the market was going up, down or sideways. I used stop losses and profit targets, and my goal was to have a winning percentage of 50%, so I just needed to be right every other trade. What a relief!

I became more relaxed. And I focused on small, but consistent profits, since now I knew the secret of Money Management.

And my day trading turned around, and so did my life:

I bought a house and we moved out of the apartment into a nice 4-bedroom house. I bought a new car and paid cash! I was less stressed, and I could finally spend more time with my family.

Life was good again!

Neighbors and friends saw that I don't go into an office and spent a lot of time with my family. So they asked what I did for a living, so I invited them into my home office and showed them. They were fascinated! They loved my simple, yet very structured approach to day trading. They told their friends about it, and more and more people started asking me to show them how to day trade. I'm was torn: I wanted to help them, show them how to trade so that they could live the lifestyle they wanted, but I spent more time teaching than day trading - and my trading started to suffer.

Rockwell Trading

With the help of my brother and my best friend, I created a website to share my knowledge. We were thinking about a name, and my sister-in-law came up with the name "Rockwell Trading." In February 2005, Rockwell Trading was founded and we published several day trading strategies. We were overwhelmed by the success: In just a few months we had become the biggest partner for Strategy Runner. Hundreds of traders were using our day trading strategies. And in early 2006, an independent company, tracking more than 1,500 trading strategies, ranked our strategies for many months in the Top Ten for "Best Futures Trading Strategies."

Our website received thousands of hits and emails were pouring in. We weren't expecting that level of demand and I have to put a team together to help me - quickly. But it was important to me that my team does what I am committed to doing: Helping traders to achieve their trading goals in a systematic way and change their lives! I wanted to make sure that every trader who comes to us gets exactly the same quality of day trading education that I gave neighbors and friends when they were sitting next to me in my home office.

Before bringing anybody on board they had to know and be fully committed to my goal:

My Vision And Goal

My goal is to help traders like you to achieve your trading goals, so that you, too, can live the lifestyle you want, afford to buy the things you want to have, be more relaxed and have more time for the things you enjoy doing, and that are important to you.

So over the years I have developed a systematic step-by-step approach that takes you from where you are today, to where you want to be. I'll give you proven day trading strategies, solid risk and money management techniques, as well as easy to use tools and techniques to control your emotions and trade with confidence and consistency.

I invite you to check out my website at www.rockwelltrading.com to check out all the resources I have for traders like you.

Looking forward to talking to you soon,

Markus Heitkoetter

Made in the USA
San Bernardino, CA
13 September 2016